Discover Big Cats

by Katrina Streza

© 2017 by Katrina Streza
ISBN: 978-1-53240-234-0
eISBN: 978-1-53240-235-7
Images licensed from Fotolia.com
All rights reserved.
No portion of this book may be reproduced
without express permission of the publisher.
First Edition
Published in the United States by
Xist Publishing
www.xistpublishing.com
PO Box 61593 Irvine, CA 92602

What makes cats special?

3

A baby lion is a cub.

Lions grow big and strong.

7

Some big cats have spots.
A Cheetah has spots.

This is a leopard. Look at the leopard's spots.

Some big cats have stripes. This white tiger has stripes.

This tiger has stripes.

Tigers can be many colors. These tiger cubs are white, black, and orange.

Some big cats have spots and stripes. This clouded leopard has spots and stripes

This lynx has spots.

This is a Lynx cub.
Look at the Lynx cub's ears.

A Lynx hunts by hearing.

25

This is a caracal.
Look at the caracal's big ears.

This is a serval.
Look at the serval's small nose.

30

This is a cougar.
Look at the cougar's big nose.

This is a panther.
Look at the panther's black fur.

www.ingramcontent.com/pod-product-compliance
Lightning Source LLC
LaVergne TN
LVHW010020070426
835507LV00001B/16